ATTRACT AND FEED A HUNGRY CROWD

How thinking like a Chef can help you build a solid business

Tea Del Alma Silvestre

FOR IRA

Thank you for the gift of space and time
to play and work and most of all, to be myself.

CONTENTS

INTRODUCTION

Remember the day you said, "Yes" to your Dream?

You hung out your shingle, launched a website and said, "Hello, World!"

There were plenty of other smart business-starting-activities, too.

You worked hard to get it right.

In all that time, bet you never said, "I can't wait to create average, boring, standard work."

Right. Neither did I.

As a way to define my business and set the stage for what was (hopefully) to come, I wrote down the basic ideas in this book. Originally, it was titled, "Be a Chef: an Entrepreneur's Manifesto."

Over the last year, I've refined these ideas and pulled them together here as a way to guide you toward creating a successful business as well as inspire you to reach for the wonderliciousness (yes, that's a word!) that is *you*.

If these keys resonate for you, please use them in your work as an entrepreneur and small business owner. And when you can, pass them on to your friends and colleagues.

ACKNOWLEDGEMENTS

Many thanks go to my inner circle, **The Blog Posse Mastermind** for their help in reviewing this manuscript:

Sharon Hurley Hall of GetPaidtoWriteOnline.com

Annie Sisk of PajamaProductivity.com

Michelle Church of VirtuallyDistinguished.com

And Nicole Fende of TheNumbersWhisperer.com

Thank you ladies for your support, encouragement and honest feedback!

Much gratitude also to Danny Iny of Firepole Marketing for generously helping me fine tune the presentation.

And most of all, to Seth Godin for the constant inspiration to reach beyond the status quo and do/be something remarkable.

CHAPTER 1: THINK LIKE A CHEF

The future belongs to chefs, not to cooks or bottle washers.
— Seth Godin, LINCHPIN

Seth Godin said it best: "The future belongs to chefs, not to cooks or bottle washers."

Was he talking about the best job prospects for the 21st century? Um, no.

He was referring to the idea that the only way to have real job security is to make yourself indispensable. To be a changemaker. To step into your superhero role and lead the world (or your neighborhood) toward something deliciously *better.*

The Chef is a metaphor for one who creates recipes, rather than follows them. As an entrepreneur, you need to think like a Chef in order to ensure your success: think creatively, work passionately and make yourself indispensable to your customers and community.

Of course, we need recipes. They help us learn the intricacies of cooking. And let's face it—entire commercial kitchens depend on them to run smoothly and crank out a consistent menu, night after night.

But behind those recipes are Chefs who create their own unique dishes.

They've learned the rules about which ingredients work (or don't work) best together. And they know how and when to deviate from those rules to get the best results.

In short, they're not afraid to tap their creativity. That's how they create new works of art.

And it's exactly what our world needs most today. **New ideas** and **new ways of thinking** around corners.

Unfortunately, there's no shortage of folks out there ready and willing to tell you exactly how to do things. "Follow this blueprint, roadmap or recipe, and you can make a million dollars in just 7 days!"

Recipes are fabulous learning tools. They help us understand new concepts so we can make them our own. They're tools that help us learn and teach others. Every Chef began their career by learning from someone else's recipe.

At some point, those same Chefs shifted gear and began experimentation, testing and research.

They *played* with their food!

Unfortunately, in business, there are gobs of sales pages selling unrealistic recipes for success. And even if the promise sounds good enough to be true, you need to remember that someone else's recipe will NOT get you the exact same results. There are just too many variables.

Variables like your particular skill set, strengths, resources, product, geographic location, target market, current political climate, ad infinitum…

If you follow someone else's path, you'll learn something (hopefully) but probably not reproduce their results. (Do I need to repeat this again?)

Better to learn the "chemistry" of how *your* ingredients interact under different circumstances. Learn which "flavors" work best together and enhance others. Learn the basics of cooking up your business so you can take that knowledge (as a framework) and create your own masterpieces.

You can absolutely do this. You *can* think like a Chef and create a remarkable small business.

Chefs are people like:

- Julia Child
- Mae West
- Rosa Parks
- Michelangelo
- Eleanor Roosevelt
- Judy Blume
- Jon Morrow
- Oscar Wilde
- Nikola Tesla
- Abraham Lincoln
- Seth Godin

and...YOU!

The way to Remarkability? Learn the recipes. Then have the courage to throw them out.

Note: The rest of this book will offer you guidelines and suggestions. Do not confuse these for recipes. Only *you* can decide the right path for your small business.

CHAPTER 2: FIND YOUR SECRET SAUCE

The secret of life? The secret's in the sauce.
— FRIED GREEN TOMATOES

Unique Selling Proposition? Nope. I'd rather call it your Secret Sauce.

Everyone (yes, everyone!) has a particular blend of talents, passions, gifts and quirkiness that make up their Secret Sauce.

As an entrepreneur, it's vitally important that you understand yours.

How? Research!

Sometimes you discover what's been there all along.

Other times, you cook it up after years of experimentation.

It's a dynamic interaction of your experiences, history and natural abilities.

Nurture it!

If you've been a freelancer or a small business owner for even a few months, I'm sure you've heard the advice, "differentiate, or die!"

The experts are like a dog with a bone: "If you want to succeed, nail down your USP" they say.

But when you're struggling to even understand what the heck a "unique selling proposition" can do for you, deciding on how to focus your marketing (via your brand) can make you feel like a lost little kid at an amusement park.

Here's my piece of advice: quit trying to discover your USP, and start cooking up your Secret Sauce.

Now you want the recipe, right?

I *knew* it.

But here's the thing: there's no one-size-fits-all, plug-and-play recipe for Secret Sauce. Nope.

Secret Sauce — by its very nature — has to be totally unlike anyone else's.

Which means, **your** recipe is something **you** have to create. (Sorry, pumpkin.)

Over the years though, I've learned that there are specific types of ingredients that every great brand uses to create their own addicting flavors.

And that is definitely something I can help you with.

Here are 9 Steps to find your Secret Sauce

Don't be fooled! These 9 steps take some time. And you'll probably need to enlist the help of a good friend or colleague to bounce some ideas around and make sure you haven't overlooked anything.

Also, you may decide to skip a step. Do whatever works for you. As long as it brings you to your goal: figuring out exactly what you bring to the table and how to communicate that in a remarkable way.

1. **Do a self-inventory:** Examine all the bits that make up who you are: your passions, values, skills, strengths, weaknesses, motivations and goals. Make lists! (You can download my free workbook for this part at http://thewordchef.com/self-inventory.)

2. **Get inside your Ideal Customer's head:** Do the same inventory that you did for yourself. Only this time, focus on who you'd really like to work with. Create an Ideal Customer persona from all that wonderful research.

3. **Find the archetypes**: Who could be the model for what you bring to the table? Is there a comic book hero, fairy tale character or real-life leader that you could say you're like? What about your ideal customer? Find one for each of you.

4. **Look for patterns**: Make a summary of your life path and employment history. Just like a fingerprint, yours is totally distinctive. Now look at the rest of what you've uncovered so far. Where are the intersections and overlaps? What kind of patterns do you see?

5. **Write the back story:** You and your ideal customer are the main characters. What big problem or desire are you two dealing with? As the hero of the story, what is your "perfect world" vision? How would you like the story to end? And, how do you champion that vision? (Hint: that's your mission statement.)

6. **Find the metaphors**: Add to the story with symbols and images. Even other words will work here. The point is to find something that your ideal customer relates to immediately. One symbol can speak volumes on your behalf. (This is where you begin to develop your business identity elements, like your logo.)

7. **Test!** How does your audience respond to this new branding? Do they get it? Do they understand the meanings behind your visual and verbal representations? And does your branding stick? (Is it memorable?)

8. **Create a plan:** Set some specific goals that you can measure and then outline how you'll reach them. What is the best way to deliver your brand's message? Is there something you can do (on a regular basis) to reinforce that message? Schedule it.

9. **Review and adjust**: Take a look every month at how your marketing (via your branding) is working for you.

Are you closing in on your goals? What do you need to adjust?

Yep, the process works.

I promise it will help you identify your particular "points of differentiation" and how to clearly express those to your target market.

I also swear on all that is holy in marketing that if you do this, you will make it 200x easier for your ideal customers to find you.

AND don't do this process in a vacuum. Get your best business friend to work through this with you. Or better yet, suggest your mastermind group tackle this over the next few weeks.

It will bring you total clarity.

CHAPTER 3: CLARITY IS POWER

I always wanted to be somebody, but I should have been more specific.
— Lily Tomlin

When you know who you are and what you're after, you don't need to hurry the process.

Clarity will show you your path and provide the momentum you need.

How do you find clarity? By doing the work (see chapter 2).

There are no short cuts. You've got to research the market, your customers and your competitors. You've got to understand the trends, opportunities and threats.

You've got to do the math and write the business plan. Only then will you know what you need to do next.

Tips for Getting to Clarity

Part of the problem (at least as I've experienced it) is a lack of time spent just *thinking*.

Most of us – myself included – get caught up in the day to day habits of go-go-go-until-your-brain-gives-up-the-ghost. And then we collapse on the couch for a couple of hours of unwinding in front of the boob tube. I do it. You do it. We all do it…way too much.

A lack of clarity is a symptom that you're not creating enough space in your days, weeks, months for considering who you are and what you want.

You may notice that time spent unplugged (like in the shower or driving the car), provides your brain with the proverbial white space to stretch and open like a flower.

You want to find more of *that*.

7 steps for getting to clarity in your work:

1. Decide that clarity is important and that you'll do whatever it takes to get there. Making that commitment is more important than all the rest of the steps combined. When you're committed to something, you'll find your own way, if you have to.

2. Set aside time *every day* – at least 30 minutes – to unplug and spend quality moments with your brain. My favorite is early in the morning, before the world comes to life. Usually that means me with a cup of coffee and a pen and paper (in case inspiration hits) cuddled up on the couch.

   If it's been a really long time since you've been alone with yourself, set up an entire day (or at least half a day). Commit to no technology. Commit to being alone and quiet. Pamper yourself just a bit with something beautiful and healthy to eat. Treat this like *a date*.

3. Ask yourself a question. Write it down. Doodle it. Let it stew for awhile on the back burner in your head. Then ask another, and another. Look at them from different angles. How do they fit together? Where are the patterns? Don't rush this. (If you keep asking, "Is it soup, yet?" you'll just bork the process.)

4. Write out your vision for a perfect world. If you could wave your magic wand and create the ultimate reality (as it relates to your product or service), what would that look like? Wiggle out the details. Visualize everything in terms of your five senses.

   This is where your business' vision comes from. (And not, "my vision is to be the premiere widget seller of all time.")

This is a vision that has to be bigger than you – something you could never create all by yourself.

Example: *My vision is a world where all small biz owners know exactly what they bring to the table and are empowered to communicate that in a joyfully delicious way.*

5. Now that you have your vision, look at your business as one of fulfilling that picture. How does your business work toward that vision? This is your mission statement. This is the purpose for why your business exists. Write that down, too.

    Example: *My mission is to help solopreneurs find and share their Secret Sauce with the world.*

6. Look at your personal values. What are your ideals? Ethics? Principles? Write these down. Now look at how you will incorporate these into your business. These will become your business' value statements.

7. Review everything you've written so far. Could you create a manifesto from this? Is everything in alignment? Does it feel *clear*? To *you*? If not, go back and play with all the ingredients again. Keep mixing and experimenting until you find just the right "click."

These steps are the ones that might get passed over when folks start a business, but they're crucial to launching from a place of clarity.

If you skipped this process in your own business, pause, breathe and spend some quality time with your heart and your brain.

You won't regret it!

CHAPTER 4: CREATE A SIGNATURE DISH

"One reason so few of us achieve what we truly want is that we never direct our focus; we never concentrate our power. Most people dabble their way through life, never deciding to master anything in particular."
— Tony Robbins

Every great Chef has a signature dish—one that defines their culinary point of view and highlights their particular skillset. Ideally, these dishes are so unique that an informed gastronome could name the chef in a blind tasting.

It's the culinary equivalent of an artist finding their own style, or an author finding their voice. In practice, a Chef's signature dish often changes with time or they may claim several signature dishes.

As a solopreneur, you need a signature dish, too. This is the **one thing** that you'll become known for (at least, initially). It will also focus your efforts and allow you to develop deep authority in a particular area, not to mention making your marketing life a whole lot easier in the process.

How do you create a signature dish? You begin with your Secret Sauce—your branding story—and then you build from there.

Here are some guidelines:

1. **Revisit your passions**. Your signature dish needs to be something you're very passionate about. Why? Because you'll be writing about it, talking about it, and sharing it with everyone *over and over and over again*. And you don't want to get bored. Choose an area that's held your fascination for at least five years, preferably more.

13

2. **Research your Ideal Customer's Wants and Needs**. What void isn't being addressed by anyone else? What questions do you keep hearing? The answers may come from your prior work with existing customers. Look back at your process for taking in a new client—do you find yourself repeating the same steps? Do they all need the same initial education on a particular issue? These are clues.

3. **Look for the intersections.** If you're a visual person, you may need to actually put everything up on the wall so you can look at it for a while. Your subconscious mind will help you, if you provide it with the relevant information. It can't help it. Our brains are wired to find patterns and categorize things. Work with that and begin to play around with different connections.

4. **Start with "Flagship" Content.** If you're a blogger, look back at your best content (sometimes referred to as your "Pillar" or "Flagship" posts) and build on this to create your signature dish.

5. **Don't be afraid of weird combinations.** Remember the old Reese's commercial? "You've got your chocolate in my peanut butter!" became a huge success precisely because people didn't expect that particular mix of ingredients.

6. **Mindmap ALL the pieces.** Do a brain dump of all the information you can possibly think of (as it relates to a possible product or program). Look at and let the bits sink in. Put it all on the backburner for a few days so your mind can continue churning the ideas around. Keep adding things as they pop up for you. When you feel pretty complete, begin to organize.

7. **Outline and Build.** Now it's time for your left brain to take over. Let it put everything into place until it begins to make real, logical sense. What's missing? What do you need to learn more about? Use this opportunity to refine your ideas. Don't edit out at this point—think BIG and let your imagination help you dream up the most delicious and enticing dish possible. There will be plenty of time for carving this up into bite-size pieces later.

8. **Name Your Dish.** This is pretty much like naming a child—you should put that much thought into it. The name should help build on your branding while also offering a promise or benefit.

9. **Test!** Don't wait for perfection here. Get your prototype out to the world and begin testing it with a small group of your ideal customers. Get their feedback. Listen to their questions and fill in the holes.

When you're ready to begin marketing your signature dish, you'll want to have a free taste you can give away as an enticement for list building purposes (and to identify future customers). Take the logical first part of your program or product and create a free gift from that.

Now, think about chunking your program or product down or out—what spin offs could you create from this signature dish? How could you offer smaller parts in a way that fuels your sales funnel and helps build long-term engagement with your Ideal Customers?

The process of creating your signature dish takes time—so don't skimp on the space you'll need to put this together (in your head, your heart and in your office).

Real, life-changing products and programs require the highest quality ingredients. Stay focused on providing the most excellent experience, but don't hold back just because something isn't quite perfect.

The only way you can make a big impact is to begin. And to keep at it every single day.

CHAPTER 5: MAKE A BIGGER PIE

What would you do if you knew you could not fail?
— ROBERT H. SCHULLER

You don't do any of us any good by holding back. And you'll certainly never be remarkable if you stay in the safe-zone.

Go out of your way to think around corners and come up with Big, Hairy Audacious Goals that scare the crap out of you.

Always keep in mind the classic question: *What would you do if you knew you could not fail?*

In 1929, during the Great Depression, the folks at the Annual Convention of Bakers got together and did just that: they baked the World's Biggest Pie. (Watch the video on YouTube: http://youtu.be/qE7gUmVHKko

Your answer is the one the Universe wants you to pursue.

Your answer is the one your heart needs you to build on.

Don't ignore them. (The Universe and Your Heart are Very Important Participants.)

Yes, the last couple of years have been a little rocky (economically speaking).

The doomsayers are happy about this. Shouting, "I told you so!" at the top of their lungs.

Some small business folks feel worried. You might be one of them. If you are, please stop for a moment and breathe.

I have a friend named Julie (not her real name). She's an entrepreneur who's worked hard over the last 6 years to build her business.

When the economy went south back in '08, she laid off her tiny staff and took care of everything herself. Then, she borrowed from her credit cards to cover some bills.

When things finally started to turn around, she was relieved. She could start to pay off that debt and put a little away again for a rainy day.

But she's been afraid to hire even one part-time person because she's *sure* the economy is going to hit bottom again before it gets better. (When our nation's credit was downgraded she said, "See?! I told you it would happen!")

My friend is tired. She's up at the crack of dawn and doesn't go home until after dinner. She feels trapped, and has no clue where to even look for that proverbial light at the end of the tunnel. She'd love to sell her business and get out, but she's convinced this isn't the right time. That she'll lose her shirt.

"And besides, what would I do? There aren't any jobs! Nobody would hire me at my age, either."

I love my friend. And I've talked her down off the ledge probably a zillion times. But as soon as I leave, she gets right back up there. Sometimes she cries. Other times she tells herself she's grateful for the tiny bit she *does* have.

Her problem? She's stuck in a world of scarcity-think. And it's stopping her from growing in a joyful way.

We've all been there. Even me.

There was a time in my early 20s when I was a single mom, buying groceries with food stamps and wondering if that child support check would arrive on time. I was so stuck in fear that most of the conversations I had literally ended with, "I can't do that. I just don't have the money."

Those were magic words. They reinforced my situation. And worst of all, I passed them on to my son.

When I finally learned that I could choose my own reactions and feelings to the events around me, I learned a valuable lesson: that **everyone creates their own experience of reality**. And the words we choose (the conversations we have, with ourselves and others) are what sets—and reinforces—our point of view. For good or ill.

If you ever want to create something remarkable with your life and your business, you need to start now to think bigger about what's possible.

Here are five good habits to help you get to that place where you can start to expand in all directions:

1. **Feed Yourself a Daily Meal of Inspiration**. Take 15 minutes (or more!) every morning to read or watch something inspirational. Ideally, this could be a chapter in a book, but could even be a blog post or a YouTube video. I really enjoy reading anything by Seth Godin (especially *Linchpin* or *Purple Cow*); but if you're looking for other ideas, check out the reading list and links at the end of this book. Those are things I've continued to find useful over the years.

2. **Join a Group of Like-minded Colleagues**. Remember when your mom worried that you were hanging out with the wrong crowd? Turns out she was right! We need the positive-reinforcement of friends and partners who can share positivity and motivation with us on a regular basis. If you're not part of a mastermind group, find or create one. This is especially crucial if you are a solopreneur like me who spends most of your time alone.

3. **Take Lots of Breaks**. When you stay at your desk or workstation for 8+ hours without changing it up, your brain gets stuck in a rut. Set a timer on your laptop or cell phone to remind you to get up, stretch, do some yoga or take a short walk. Not only is this healthier for

you, it will allow different synapses in your brain to fire —and possibly let in some brilliant inspiration. I usually get my best ideas in the shower or when I'm out for a walk.

4. **Make an Appointment with Your Creative, CEO-Self**. If you ever want to think about the future of your business and how to make it better, you've got to set aside time to be the CEO. Get out of your office and go somewhere different. Turn off your cell phone. Just bring a small notebook and a pen. Ideally, this would be a 60-min block of time, once a week for dreaming about new products, services or collaborations. Ask yourself a lot of "What if…?" questions. And then write down your answers.

5. **Set Big Hairy Audacious Goals**. Ever heard of the BHAG? It's a huge goal that excites you and makes you nervous at the same time. It's something that if you pull off, would create an enormous impact on you and others. It's risky, but worth it. And best of all, it won't allow you to stay stuck in scarcity think!

I'm not saying you should ignore the events around you. Instead, I invite you to change your thoughts about them so you don't get stuck.

So instead of worrying about whether you're going to get a big enough slice of the economic pie, be different! Bake a whole new pie. Something bigger and better than everyone else expects. And then share it liberally with everyone you meet.

CHAPTER 6: SHARE GENEROUSLY

I am what I am because of who we all are.
— UBUNTU PHILOSOPHY

Relationships. Are. Everything. (Say it with me.)

In my humble opinion, they're the *only* thing that matters.

Every story exists in relationship to everything else around it. So share! We are all ONE anyway.

This is also an important way to approach business.

Share your recipes. Vanessa Pagan points out that "the difference between the famous chefs like Julia Child and Emeril Lagasse and their unknown and equally great counterparts is that the famous ones **"out-share, out-teach and out-contribute."** In her post, "Follow the Chefs: Marketing in a Crowded Industry," Pagan explains that:

> Famous chefs have cookbooks, cooking shows on local networks, cable channels or YouTube clips. Famous chefs teach regular people at home how to use the same recipes and make the same foods that they serve at their restaurants and in their homes. They passionately want their audience to follow along and create the same dishes because they are lifting the curtain on how to cook delicious foods and giving away their secrets and styles on cooking.

Giving away their methodologies hasn't hurt their bottom lines. It's actually helped build relationships between the chefs and their audience. Relationships that translate into enormous brand empires in the billions of dollars. Folks buy everything from prepared foods to cookware from their favorite celebrity chefs— not to mention visiting their restaurants in droves.

Lesson: Give away your best content. Formal marketing and advertising doesn't work anymore. It's time to teach and share.

And while you're sharing, remember that every action you take will nurture (or kill) a business relationship.

Here are 38 real-world ways to share yourself and nurture your connections:

Online AND Off

1. **Take responsibility when you screw up**. We all make mistakes, but when you don't own up to yours, it makes you look immature and unprofessional.

2. **Give proper credit when it's due**. People know whose idea or hard work went into something. Or they'll find out. Think twice before you leave out important details — like who's really responsible for that great thing that happened.

3. **Reveal just enough of your personal life**. I don't need to know all the sordid details but please be willing to share a little. It's how we get to know each other and build rapport.

4. **Treat everyone as equals**. Of course we have different levels and types of relationships. But if I see you treating a colleague or peer differently than you treat me, it's gonna affect the way I ultimately treat you. The same goes for other types of business relationships.

5. **Be willing and able to pay full price**. If we give a friends-and-family-discount to everyone we're friends with, we'd have to file bankruptcy. Never start a business relationship from a place of entitlement.

6. **Keep your promises**. Don't tell me you can do something if you know you can't do it. Yes, sometimes things happen. But when it happens multiple times, the pattern gets noticed.

7. **Start from "How can I help *you*?"** I would love to help you with your project, cause, etc. IF it's a good fit for me personally and professionally. But if you ask for help more than you offer it, I will begin to feel used.

8. **Tell the truth**. Most people may not have a BS meter that's 100% foolproof, but we can usually tell when we're not getting the whole truth. Little white lies, too. Just be honest.

9. **Be direct**. If you've got something to say, just say it. A direct answer says volumes about you and what you care about.

10. **Talk to the source when something's wrong**. Complaining to those other than the one who can help you, usually won't get you anywhere. And there's the possibility you've jumped to conclusions about what really happened. Whatever it was, you can usually clear things up by having a conversation.

11. **Share the good stuff about other people's products and services**. You might not want to talk about mine (um, why?) but share the good that you see in the world. When you only talk about your own products and services, you let people know you're just showing up to show off *you*.

12. **Let me bow out gracefully**. No means no. Simple as that.

13. **Make me look fabulous for referring you**. When I make a referral, I'm putting my reputation on the line. If you screw up, you may have killed the trust I had built with that person. And conversely, when you shine, we all shine ten times brighter.

14. **Share your network**. We all know someone who should be introduced to someone in our network. Being generous with your network shows that you're a connector and someone to know.

15. **Be willing to participate**. In the conversation, the cause or the community. If you join a group, and you don't participate, why are you there?

16. **Share bad news sparingly**. Nobody likes to hear they have spinach in their teeth, but if you're a good friend, you'll tell them. On the flip side, if you've *always* got something or someone to complain about (especially your customers or competitors), how do I know you won't complain about me, too?

17. **Walk the talk**. Ever seen someone tell their clients to do one thing, and then not do it themselves? Doesn't make you feel all warm and fuzzy inside about them, am I right?

18. **Don't be *too* nice or helpful**. There's a point where you cross over into schmoozeville. Be careful! Don't get weird and stalkerish.

19. **Communicate your expectations**. People who don't communicate their opinions, desires and needs make it really hard to work with them. Don't be afraid to tell people who you are, where you stand and what works best for you. Especially in a client/vendor relationship.

20. **Have a little faith in your new relationships**. Give people the benefit of the doubt until they prove they're not worthy. People should have to earn your distrust. Yes, trust your gut. But if you're overly paranoid about something, you'll make it difficult for people to feel safe about a relationship with you.

21. **Stay in touch with those who knew you "when."** If you've recently hit the big time (or have just started to find real success), you're going to be busy. But stay mindful of those who helped get you where you are now. If you decide you no longer have time for those of us who "knew you when" you'll create a lot of hard feelings. Find a way to stay in touch.

22. **Be willing to delegate**. As you grow, you will *need* to learn to hire the right team members (and then trust them to get the job done). There's only so much that one person can do. Don't be the person who kills their business before it really gets started because you can't delegate. Get yourself an assistant (virtual or otherwise).

23. **Keep confidences**. If someone tells you something—unless they say otherwise—always assume it was meant for your ears only. And don't share something with me about someone else just because you think you're safe. If you do this often, I will stop talking to you about my own challenges.

24. **Pull your weight**. Team efforts require everyone's energy. If you can't or won't give it all you've got, it's nearly the same as taking credit for other peoples' work. Ew.

25. **The process is just as important as the product**. Before you take one more shortcut or cut one more corner, ask yourself, "would I be proud to put this piece of work in my portfolio?"

In-Person

26. **Look me in the eye**. I know in some cultures it's offensive, but in the West, eye contact tells me you want to connect. Plus, your body language speaks volumes. If you're fidgeting, I'll definitely pick up on that. Relax and breathe. We're both just people.

27. **Give me your full attention when we're talking**. Listening is huge. If you can't give me your full attention, why should I give you mine?

28. **Make appointments, don't just pop in**. Unless you're my honey, or my BFF, showing up unannounced might not be the best idea. We're all very busy people, and it's foolish to expect folks to just drop everything to help you. Call first. Let's make a mutually-convenient appointment.

29. **Keep your appointments**. If you ask for an appointment and then don't show (and even worse, you don't call), then you're telling that person you either a) don't really care about the relationship, or b) you don't have the organizational skills to keep it together. Pick one.

30. **Be on time**. And yes, call if you'll be late. (See notes on #29, above).

31. **Don't answer your cell phone when we're meeting**. Especially if we're at a restaurant! Need to brush up on your cell phone etiquette?[1]

Online

32. **Share who you are.** This is especially true on your website. If you don't want to talk about yourself even just a little, I may think you don't want me to know who you are.

33. **Send well written emails**. Your grammar doesn't need to be 100%, but if you refuse to take the time to capitalize (or, if you over-capitalize) it tells me you don't want to take the time to communicate properly. That you don't care. (See the footnotes for some great tips for writing better emails.[2])

34. **Use a branded email account for your business**. Take 15 minutes to set up your email so it matches your website (or have someone else do it for you). This tells the world that you've made a real commitment to your business. That you're a professional. Check with your domain registrar or web hosting service on how to do this.

35. **Reply to your emails and phone calls**. Yes, you're busy, so if you can't give a full response, let folks know. You should respond to every email and phone call within 24 to 48 hours. Or hire someone to help you. Period.

36. **Only add people to your email list with their permission**. There's this thing called SPAM…and yep, there's a law about it, too. Just because you've got

[1] http://techtips.salon.com/etiquette-cell-phone-use-3881.html

[2] http://www.101emailetiquettetips.com/

my email address doesn't mean I want your newsletter. Or your sales pitches.

37. **Add your phone number and/or your mailing address to your website**. Don't you want people to connect with you? It's okay if you don't have a mailing address, as long as you've got at least a phone number. (Although, I won't be able to send you my handwritten thank you cards if you don't include a mailing address.) But using *only* an email form as the way to communicate is a sure way to keep your potential customers from trusting you.

38. **Use a real name/photo**. Yes, the internet can be a scary place. But if you don't use your photo, or your name, how will we ever get to know each other? This is especially true on Twitter. If you want to work under a nom de plume, okay—but choose something other than cutegirl360.

Remember, words are important. But it's *our actions* and how we deliver those words that speak the truth about who we are. Some of these will be more or less hurtful to your relationships than others.

Yes, you're human. And yes, you'll screw up. But stay vigilant about slipping up with a new relationship. It can kill things for you before you even get started.

For me, relationships are really all that matter. Yes, your bottom line is important. But without relationships, you won't have a bottom line to worry about.

And relationships are all about how we communicate.

CHAPTER 7: WORDS ARE MAGIC INGREDIENTS

Words are our most inexhaustible source of magic. They are our most potent forms of enchantment. Rich with the power to hurt or heal.
– Dumbledore, HARRY POTTER AND THE DEATHLY HALLOWS

Words really do have magic in them. Use them only for good.

Learn everything you can about their power and how they help us manifest what we're after.

Never twist the truth or use words to generate fear or other negative emotions.

And then? Put your words together in a way that makes us *feel something.*

Even one sentence can tell a story. Here's an example:

For sale: baby shoes, never worn.

Those six words were written by Hemingway. (And he often referred to it as his best work!)

When you read that sentence, your brain takes in the information and begins to fill out the details surrounding it. If you're the sensitive type, you might even get teary-eyed.

For centuries, our species has believed that words have a certain magical power. That you could cast a spell by using the right words, causing or commanding the natural elements to do your bidding.

Today, most of us would agree that words definitely influence behavior. Quantum physics aside, we've got highly trained professionals in the fields of Neurolinguistic Programming (NLP), hypnosis, and of course, advertising — who all understand the true power of words.

Some words are more powerful than others, to be sure. Words like *free*, and *guarantee* are two that we know make strong connections and command attention from readers.

Remember my story from Chapter four? How I talked about my time as a young single mother, living on food stamps? How I reinforced my situation with constant use of the phrase, "I can't afford it." – and how I passed that world view on to my young son?

It took us both some time, but we turned those thoughts around. He is now a young man, attending a prestigious art school in Southern California. He thinks big about his future most every day ("There's an internship at Pixar waiting for me, Mom.") And even though the price tag for his education could pay off the debt for a small country, he's committed to making it work. To following his dreams.

His story is just getting started. And it's the self-talk that he chooses that will help or hinder his progress.

The words he chooses to describe his situation are determining – minute by minute – his experience of his own life.

But guess what? Those words are empty phrases. Words alone don't really have any magical power. It's actually the emotion behind them that matters. And emotions are best conveyed (to ourselves and others) via stories.

Chip and Dan Heath, the authors of *Made to Stick*, point out that stories help our brains remember and understand new concepts better than dry descriptions, facts and figures.

Case studies and articles are great examples of where marketing stories show up. But you can include smaller vignettes on your

About Us page, your Facebook posts, or even in your tweets! Literally, everywhere.

Here are 5 elements to include in your story-messages:

1. **Emotion**. Choose something that will connect with your target audience. If you've done your research and understand your ideal customer, you'll know which emotions they're already dealing with as it pertains to your offering. If they're mostly frustrated, use that emotion in your story.

2. **Vivid, concrete images**. Help your reader visualize what's happening (or what could happen) by describing a particular moment in detail.

3. **A surprise or mystery**. Capture your reader's attention by playing on their curiosity in your title or headline. And help them remember your story better by including an unexpected twist at the end.

4. **Simplicity**. Not just short, but direct and to the point. With too many twists and turns, you'll confuse your reader and ultimately lose their attention.

5. **Credibility**. Don't go overboard with the description. Your story needs to sound like it really could happen in order for people to believe and trust you.

Tell us stories that matter and have meaning and you'll be sure to create a remarkable business.

CHAPTER 8: WE EAT WITH OUR EYES FIRST

Everyone needs beauty as well as bread.
-- John Muir, AUTHOR

Before anyone ever decides to read a word of your website or marketing materials, they first need to be comfortable and enticed with how things *look*.

Chefs understand this. They take great joy in arranging the food on a plate. They know that presentation counts. Colors, textures and even the quantity of food helps create an unforgettable dining experience.

If the food is just heaped on the plate willy nilly, the guest might lose her appetite. Or she might feel that she just wasn't worth the Chef's trouble.

That's certainly no way to start off a meal.

As individuals, we're also judged on how we look, how we present ourselves.

If we dress like hippies, we probably won't fit in on Wall Street (and vice versa).

And just as we're assessed by how we present ourselves as people, our business is judged by how it "dresses itself," too.

Often, a potential customer's first interaction with your company is via your marketing materials.

What does your website say about who you are as a business?

Is it visually appealing? Organized?

If you want to attract more people to your party, set a beautiful table. Don't skimp. Get out the good china and use your best silver. Don't be satisfied with "good enough."

Here are 5 things to consider as you create the visuals of your marketing :

1. **Consider your guest's preferences**. Know who you're trying to communicate with and understand them inside and out. This will help you create something beautiful and appealing to the right people.

2. **Design your logo as the visual symbol of who you are and what you stand for.** Just like your handwriting speaks volumes about your personality, the typeface you choose tells the world about your brand's personality.

    Are you a traditional, steadfast kind of business? Then you'll want to look at fonts that use serifs (the ones with feet, like the font used for the body copy of this book). Serifs demonstrate a certain groundedness or ability to stay upright.

    Or is your business a fresh new face with lots of optimism? Then you'll probably want something sans serif (without the feet) and a little bit rounded with lots of space between the letters.

    In any case, pick a font (no more than two) that help tell your brand story. You don't have to be a handwriting analyst in order to figure some of this out, but you should at least confer with a knowledgeable graphic designer.

3. **Convey mood and personality through color**. Be sure to choose your colors with thought and purpose. The guideline is to stick with two colors (not counting black or white). This will help your ideal customers remember you best.

4. **Choose the best images you can afford.** Especially if you sell a product. Good photography will go miles toward telling the world you mean business. This goes for any image—photograph or illustration—that you use on your website or in your marketing. And if you don't sell a product? Then get professional photos taken of you and your team. As a service professional, you *are* the product.

5. **Keep things consistent.** This means deciding early on how you'll use the various visual elements and then ensuring you (and your team) adhere to those decisions. You're the Chef here, so you decide. Put your masterpiece together and then write down the recipe so others can follow your lead. This recipe is your style guide and it's important to document your decisions – even if you're the only one moving the ingredients around.

   Having a style guide doesn't necessarily mean you can't ever change things, though. The great thing about websites is that unlike printed materials, you can make continuous improvements (little tweaks over time) without breaking the bank. Just don't make too many changes, too quickly, or you'll confuse your audience.

Quality images, appropriate amounts of white space, and the right color scheme can go a long way toward enticing your guests to eat what you're serving.

And when you've done all that, go back and ask yourself how you could make it even more enticing. Your table settings should evolve over time. This isn't a once-and-done kind of thing.

If you're not great with design, hire someone who is. Make sure it's someone you like and trust, who has references and a good reputation. Choose someone who thinks of your project as a collaboration, and you'll go far.

CHAPTER 9: COLLABORATE IN THE KITCHEN

*I never did anything alone. Whatever was accomplished
in this country was accomplished collectively.*
— Golda Meir, PRIME 4ᵀᴴ MINISTER OF ISRAEL

Be open and willing to engage with other Chefs. The energy and ideas you can create together will be exponentially more exciting than what you can do on your own.

Don't think of your competition as the enemy. They are just a different iteration of you. Work with them. Contrary ideas can create fabulous new "purple cows."

Have you ever tried to do something big? No, I mean, massively huge — something even a little audacious? (See Chapter Four)

If you haven't, you're missing out on one of the best adventures of your life.

But if you have, then you know you can't really pull off something ginormous without the help of other people. It changes regular math so that $1 + 1 + 1 = 300$!

Here's a story about one woman who did just that...

Colleen Wainwright (aka The Communicatrix) had a pivotal birthday in September of 2011, but she began thinking about it much, much earlier.

She told me it was so she could psych herself up for the big occasion. In January of 2010, she started mulling over the fact that she would be 50 sooner than she'd like. And over the course of that year, an idea about how to really mark the occasion started to take form: she would raise $50,000 in 50 days for a worthy nonprofit.

WriteGirl became the recipient of her largesse after a friend of hers pointed out the obvious connection between their mission and who Colleen is in this world. (As Colleen, says: *Duh.*)

From there, things started to snowball and after months of planning, she launched an online campaign.

At the end of her campaign, she not only reached her goal, she surpassed it, raising $61,517 in personal donations and another $50,000 in a matching grant (total = $111,517!).

{ To read more about Colleen's fabulous collaboration, visit http://50for50.us/blog/ }

How did she pull off this massive awesomeness? Here are some lessons she shared with me:

1. **Pick a cause that connects with who you are.** You have to align with YOUR particular passion. It needs to be real. It needs to be something you can "care a whole lot about in front of everybody." Colleen is a writer. And she's a woman who cares about other women. She also loves what WriteGirl is about and has supported them in little ways for a while now, so it was a natural fit to make them the focus of this campaign.

2. **Be authentic.** It will inspire others. (Colleen's authenticity has inspired me for years.) There's always room to inject your story into the project. It's when you let some of your real self show, that others get interested. But do it in a structured way. You don't need to show up in your "Sunday-go-to-meetin' clothes, but don't show up in your boxer shorts either!" Being real helps attract the right people and build your community.

3. **Put together a team.** Don't try this alone! Get your closest friends on board first, and then look around for a few more of the right people to partner with. It's not

about quantity, it's about quality. You don't have to have a huge tribe to make a difference, just a few, *really* committed and loyal audience members. Oh yeah, who really believe in you and get what you're doing. Give them something they can take to their networks and pass on. (For more on this topic, see Kevin Kelly's post on a 1000 True Fans.)[3]

4. **It's not about you. It's about everybody.** Find ways to help everyone participate and make it about them. When you have a mission that's not about you (or at least not just about you), you're way more likely to get people to engage — to share your thing and pass it on. And the Bonus? The joy you'll get back from your efforts will be 100x bigger than the amount of work you put into it. What's better than feeling great because you've done good?

5. **Don't over think it.** You can mull the project over for a while and you should let your ideas stew a bit, but don't get stuck in over-planning. When you're ready, talk with your closest allies and bounce your ideas off of them. This is part of good preparation. And of course, talk with some experts and see if you've covered your bases. But then, ACT. Put one foot in front of the other and have faith that all of your preparation will help make it come together. If something goes wrong, take it in stride and adjust around it.

6. **Get really clear on the WHAT and the WHY.** You need to figure out your story before you start talking about it in public. In Colleen's case, she had to figure out the answer to the question, "Why do you have to shave your head? How does that fit into this project?" (Listen to the podcast to find out![4])

7. **Say Thank You.** Be generous and acknowledge that folks are participating by giving them something back.

---

[3] http://www.kk.org/thetechnium/archives/2008/03/1000_true_fans.php

[4] http://www.blogtalkradio.com/wordchef/2011/07/29/colleen-wainwright-invites-the-world-to-her-50th-b-day

Colleen's got this part down, too. Not only did I get thank you goodies for my donation, but she sent me a handwritten note right afterwards. Gratitude is rocket fuel for anything you do—especially when you're involving others.

8. **Evaluate as you go**. Not just about how the project's coming along. (Act like Wiley E. Coyote: make adjustments if you have to, and keep trying.) But also notice what you're learning about yourself, your friends, the world. What do the various pieces of the pie mean to you? To others? Pay attention to what happens and you'll keep the momentum going and building to a smashing crescendo.

That's the power of collaborating. In this case, it was a world-wide online collaboration. Colleen showed us that collaboration creates something exponentially larger than the elements you start with.

What about for-profit collaborations? Glad you asked. (Read on!)

10 Types of Collaborations that Build Brands

1. **Blog Tribes.** You may also know these as "blog alliances." The idea is simple (and not necessarily easy): find other serious, quality bloggers with strong brands of their own, who write for the same target audience that you do. Commit to sharing and commenting on each other's blog posts. As you work together, everyone's individual brands help support and give credibility to your brand (and vice versa).

   Blog tribes are structured in many different ways. Some loosely, some more formally. And some (via tools like Triberr.com) utilize technology to make the sharing easier.

   The blog tribe I work with is a fabulous bunch of writers who work together as "carnies" in our monthly Word Carnivals. (Note: new carney blood is always good.

Check out what we're looking for at WordCarnivals.com.)

2. **Masterminds.** These groups are powerful alliances between peers. The purpose is to help support and enlighten each other on the road to success. However, it's much more than a support group for like-minded people. Mastermind groups bring together individuals who share the same goals and dreams and work together to achieve them.

    Some of the Word Carnival bloggers decided to work together even more closely, so we formed a mastermind group we call the Blog Posse. We "meet" twice monthly by phone and have a private Facebook Group where we share each other's posts, ask for help with business and personal challenges, and provide ongoing encouragement and support to each other. I love this group because it gives me my own Board of Advisors or 'Brain Trust' to keep me on track with my business goals, and more.

    For more on masterminds, check out *Meet and Grow Rich*, by Vitale and Hibbler.

3. **Marketing Cooperatives**. These bring together a group of businesses that all have a common thread: a location, an industry, or a target market. The group pools its resources (usually money) to leverage the power of the whole. For example, you might not be able to afford a good radio advertising campaign on your own, but if the entire shopping center pitches in, you'd have enough to buy some decent spots that promoted everyone. Here's a great article[5] on how to create a marketing cooperative.

4. **Sponsorships**. These involve a trade of money or other resources in exchange for exposure. If you live on Planet Earth, you already know how these work. The idea is to sponsor something (usually an event) that will get you some exposure to the folks who attend the event.

5. **Staff Collaborations**. If you're lucky enough to have an official team of paid staff, be sure that everyone is on the

---

[5] http://www.ehow.com/how_4524668_start-business-marketing-coop.html

same page about the brand. This is especially true for the front line folks who come in contact with your customers. Each interaction with the customer is a chance to build the brand. So hire the right people, train them, and keep them inspired and loyal.

6. **Product/Service Collaborations.** Build a new product with one or more partners. You can innovate something new and awesome when you bring together different types of expertise. These types of collaborations are usually termed Joint Ventures (and generally involve lawyers and contracts). They can be tricky, but when they work — pow!

    If you're a service provider, consider working with one or more partners. If you do web design, you might work with someone who does copy writing on the same project. When you find other service providers who rock what they do, hold onto those relationships! It could be mutually beneficial for you to band together to offer all-in-one or bundled options. In the past, we might have called this "subcontracting," but that doesn't really capture the true spirit of what a collaboration between peers can do. These can also be formal (with contracts) or informal and work more as referral partnerships.

7. **Virtual Teams**. When you start to grow your business, don't wait to hire outside help. You might not be ready for a full-fledged employee, but you should definitely get a virtual assistant if you find yourself being less responsive to existing customers. This is probably one of THE most important things you'll need to do to create a solid brand: especially if you want to maintain your reputation! I've literally seen dozens of people lose valuable clients because they failed to get help when things started to get busy.

    And VAs aren't the only types of virtual team members you'll need. Don't forget a bookkeeper, an IT professional, a CPA, an attorney, and of course a marketing expert. Depending on your business type and model, you'll need to collaborate with a myriad of professionals until you're big enough to hire them permanently. Failing to find and work with the right support, will be disastrous to your brand.

8. **Referral Partnerships**. Groups like BNI and other networks have been doing this for years, but you can also create your own.

   Start by making a list of every type of service or product that your ideal customer might want or need (start with those just related to your industry, and then work out in concentric circles until you feel like you've captured everything).

   Search out and build relationships with those types of businesses. Start slowly, and over time (as you feel confident referring the business), you can work on more elaborate or formal ways to exchange leads, or even monetize them (pay commissions).

   One great example of how to do this is by using Gift Certificates: You create a gift certificate for something of real value in your business (worth at least $100 or more). It can't be $100 off. It needs to be for something totally FREE. Your referral partner does the same. You exchange an equal amount of gift certificates with each other and then pass them on to the appropriate customers. You could further incentivize each other by offering a commission if that person becomes a long time customer.

   Basically, anytime you work together to share leads—in any format—you've got a referral partnership. If you're looking to do something really big (like a product launch), and you aren't connected to the A-list crowd, you might want to consider working with a JV broker.

9. **Your Local Community**. Every business—even those online—exists in a community. Your community benefits from your existence. If you're locally based, it's easier to see how this works (especially if you collect and pay taxes). But even if your small business serves the entire planet, there is still a community that benefits from having you there. Think about the community of music

lovers—some might argue they benefit from the existence of iTunes.

The idea here is to enlist them as partners in all areas of your brand building. How? By getting involved! Join a special interest group and participate. Be a giver of advice and information, but also seek out advice and information from the other members. If your community has an official umbrella, be sure to weave your association with them into your marketing (even if it's just on your About page). You'll both benefit from that exposure.

10. **Your Customers**. Involve your clients in all aspects of your business, but especially product development and promotion. Seek out their advice on what improvements might be made to your product or how you deliver it (services are products, too). And make it easy for them to help promote you to their friends and colleagues. But don't forget about customer to customer collaboration! Build opportunities into your business for your customers to work together and you'll be on your way to building a community!

The key with all of these, is to find collaborators with strong brands of their own.

Their brand + your brand (must) = Awesomeness[3]

You can begin with just three individuals. If all of you really *bring it* (in the truest sense of that phrase), you'll create something that ripples out beyond the horizon of where it started—something really beautiful and life-changing for people you don't even know.

What an adventure!

CHAPTER 10: FEED US HEROIC STORIES

A hero is someone who has given his or her life to something bigger than oneself.
-- Joseph Campbell, AUTHOR

Stories are food.

Feed everyone. And be willing to let them feed you (listen!).

Remember humans love stories—it's hardwired into how we learn and grow.

Why did you start your business? That's a story.

Who are your best customers? That's another story.

How does your product work? That's an entirely different story.

But in order for us to hear them as stories, you need to show us with a narrative. You've got to utilize characters—heroes and villains. You must touch our emotions.

Let's start with characters. Every story has a hero.

And in nearly every story, the hero's journey is one of adventure, intrigue and deep learning that benefits all of humanity.

You're already the hero of your story. *Own that.*

What obstacles or challenges have you already overcome? What lessons have you learned?

Share those with your customers and prospects. Let people see your heroic human side.

And speaking of your customers, every hero has a side-kick. Your customers are just like side-kicks. They want the same thing you want. You're working together to vanquish the same challenges (aka, the villains). Make sure they understand their role as it relates to the overall plot.

And yes, your story must have a *plot*.

How do you know if your story has a plot?

Consider these two narratives:

There once was a king and a queen. The king died and then the queen died.

There once was a king and a queen. The king died. And then the queen died of a broken heart.

Which one tells you a story? That's the one with the plot.

How do you add this sort of element to your business stories? By focusing on emotion.

Don't just talk about features and benefits. Dig deeper and find the underlying emotional benefits for those features.

If you're selling lipstick, your product's features might be things like its color, its price, or even that it contains a secret ingredient.

So what? Those are your characters. What do they *do*? And more importantly, *why should we care?*

That lipstick's color might be an exclusive new shade of red developed for the Queen of England. It might be a longer-lasting red. Or it might be a red that magically matches your skin tone.

Still, I ask you—*so what?*

The woman who buys that lipstick and chooses it for its color is most likely doing so because she believes it will improve her appearance. Maybe even make her *beautiful.*

Why is it important to know this?

Because the emotion behind that purchase is *hope.* And if you include some of that in your marketing, you'll be more likely to connect with your prospective customer—and she'll remember you when it's time to buy a new lipstick.

The stories we tell literally create our businesses. Learn how to tell them.

Use them to describe how your product or service is different. Use them to teach your prospects something new.

Use them to inspire change—in your customers and in the world.

Step into and embrace your inner Hero-Chef. Lean towards YES.

"Yes, I can do this. Yes, this will be challenging but we can do this. Yes, I'm taking this on. Yes, I can see a better way!"

When you share this side of yourself in public, you give others an example and inspire them to step out and take risks, too.

Most people put limitations around what they believe they can and cannot do. They give up too easily.

They listen to the inner critic (another villain) who tells them their work is below par or just plain baloney. They don't understand that everyone's first attempt at anything is usually a big pile of crap.

As the hero, it's your job to remember (and to remind others) that in this Universe, literally *anything is possible.*

When you know that—when you embrace all possibilities—you'll find the courage to seek out new experiences and turn things on their ear when the moment calls for it.

You'll also give the rest of us a reason to keep trying.

The status quo doesn't need your help. Our world craves visionaries and innovators and people who aren't afraid to forge new paths. We need you to create an epic tale with your life that inspires us all to reach beyond mediocrity.

Our world needs your business to be remarkable. To change things up and make things better.

Be our Hero-Chef!

READING LIST

I love to read (duh). And when I'm not reading supernatural romances, I'm devouring nonfiction business and self-improvement titles. (Amazon loves me!)

The following list encompasses some of my favorite, and most recommended titles in the field of marketing. Some of these are classics that I've recommended for years. And others are fairly new—they're in no particular order. The one thing they all have in common: solid advice and information you need in order to market successfully. Enjoy!

Engagement from Scratch!: How Super-Community Builders Create a Loyal Audience and How You Can Do the Same! by Danny Iny, C.C. Chapman, Mitch Joel, Natalie Sisson, Corbett Barr, Danny Brown, Brian Clark, Derek Halpern, Gini Dietrich, Dino Dogan, Evan Carmichael, Guy Kawasaki, Randy Komisar, Kristi Hines, Jeff Bullas, Sean Platt, Mark W. Schaefer, Marcus Sheridan, Adam Toren, Anita Campbell, Alexander Osterwalder

Brainfluence: 100 Ways to Persuade and Convince Consumers with Neuromarketing by Roger Dooley

The New Relationship Marketing: How to Build a Large, Loyal, Profitable Network Using the Social Web by Mari Smith

Trust Agents: Using the Web to Build Influence, Improve Reputation, and Earn Trust by Chris Brogan, Julien Smith

It's Not What You Sell, It's What You Stand For: Why Every Extraordinary Business Is Driven by Purpose by Roy M. Spence Jr., Haley Rushing

Book Yourself Solid: The Fastest, Easiest, and Most Reliable System for Getting More Clients Than You Can

Handle Even if You Hate Marketing and Selling by Michael Port

Beyond Booked Solid: Your Business, Your Life, Your Way–It's All Inside by Michael Port

Tribes: We Need You to Lead Us by Seth Godin

Purple Cow, New Edition: Transform Your Business by Being Remarkable by Seth Godin

Linchpin: Are You Indispensable? by Seth Godin

All Marketers are Liars (with a New Preface): The Underground Classic That Explains How Marketing Really Works–and Why Authenticity Is the Best Marketing of All by Seth Godin

Blue Ocean Strategy: How to Create Uncontested Market Space and Make Competition Irrelevant by W. Chan Kim, Renee Mauborgne

The Thank You Economy by Gary Vaynerchuk

Enchantment: The Art of Changing Hearts, Minds, and Actions by Guy Kawasaki

Launch: How to Quickly Propel Your Business Beyond the Competition by Michael A. Stelzner

Content Rules: How to Create Killer Blogs, Podcasts, Videos, Ebooks, Webinars (and More) That Engage Customers and Ignite Your Business (New Rules Social Media Series) by Ann Handley, C.C. Chapman

Made to Stick: Why Some Ideas Survive and Others Die by Chip Heath and Dan Heath

Guerrilla Marketing (any of his books) by Jay Conrad Levinson

The E-Myth Revisited (not strictly marketing but uber important) by Michael E. Gerber

The Ultimate Sales Machine: Turbocharge Your Business with Relentless Focus on 12 Key Strategies by Chet Holmes

The Idea Writers: Copywriting in a New Media and Marketing Era (Advertising Age) by Teressa Iezzi

Web Copy That Sells: The Revolutionary Formula for Creating Killer Copy That Grabs Their Attention and Compels Them to Buy by Maria Veloso

Invisible Ink: A Practical Guide to Building Stories that Resonate by Brian McDonald

Buyology: Truth and Lies About Why We Buy by Martin Lindstrom

Brandwashed: Tricks Companies Use to Manipulate Our Minds and Persuade Us to Buy by Martin Lindstrom

The Power of Unpopular: A Guide to Building Your Brand for the Audience Who Will Love You (and why no one else matters) by Erika Napoletano

When you're done reading all these great books, check out what's new at HungryCrowdBook.com. I'll be adding some delicious tools and resources (free to download) to help you take advantage of all this good advice.

ABOUT THE AUTHOR

Tea (sounds like Tay'ah) Silvestre, aka The Word Chef, is a recovering English major with a passion for all things gastronomic and a (totally *not* weird) WordPress fetish.

She's also the founder of the Tastiest Small Biz Brand Award and the host of The Word Café (blogtalkradio.com/wordchef) podcast on BlogTalkRadio.

She coaches solopreneurs everywhere on how to find and share their Secret Sauce with the world.

The Word Chef Headquarters are currently based in Silicon Valley, California and share valuable real estate with Tea and Mr. Spouse, Ira.

She invites you to contact her via email with questions or comments: tea@thewordchef.com, connect with her on Twitter @teasilvestre or visit her site at theWordChef.com.

www.ingramcontent.com/pod-product-compliance
Lightning Source LLC
Chambersburg PA
CBHW071633170526
45166CB00003B/1309